IMAGES
of England

WHITLEY BAY

St Mary's Island became such a popular landmark that it was adopted for the badge of Whitley and Monkseaton Council. When the lighthouse was decommissioned it was preserved by North Tyneside Council.

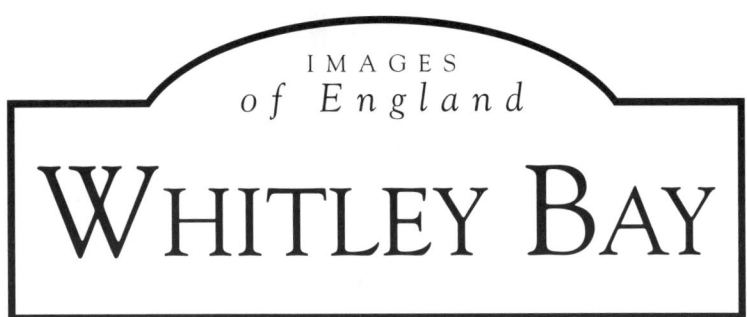

IMAGES
of England

WHITLEY BAY

Compiled by
Eric Hollerton

TEMPUS

First published 1999
Reprinted 1999, 2001
Copyright © Eric Hollerton, 1999

Tempus Publishing Limited
The Mill, Brimscombe Port,
Stroud, Gloucestershire, GL5 2QG

ISBN 0 7524 1179 9

Typesetting and origination by
Tempus Publishing Limited
Printed in Great Britain by
Midway Clark Printing, Wiltshire

Cover picture: Sandcastle competition, 14 July 1909. Norah Davy, of 32 South Parade, was an enthusiastic competitor. It is believed in the family that the competitions ended because the Davy girls were such frequent prize winners.

Contents

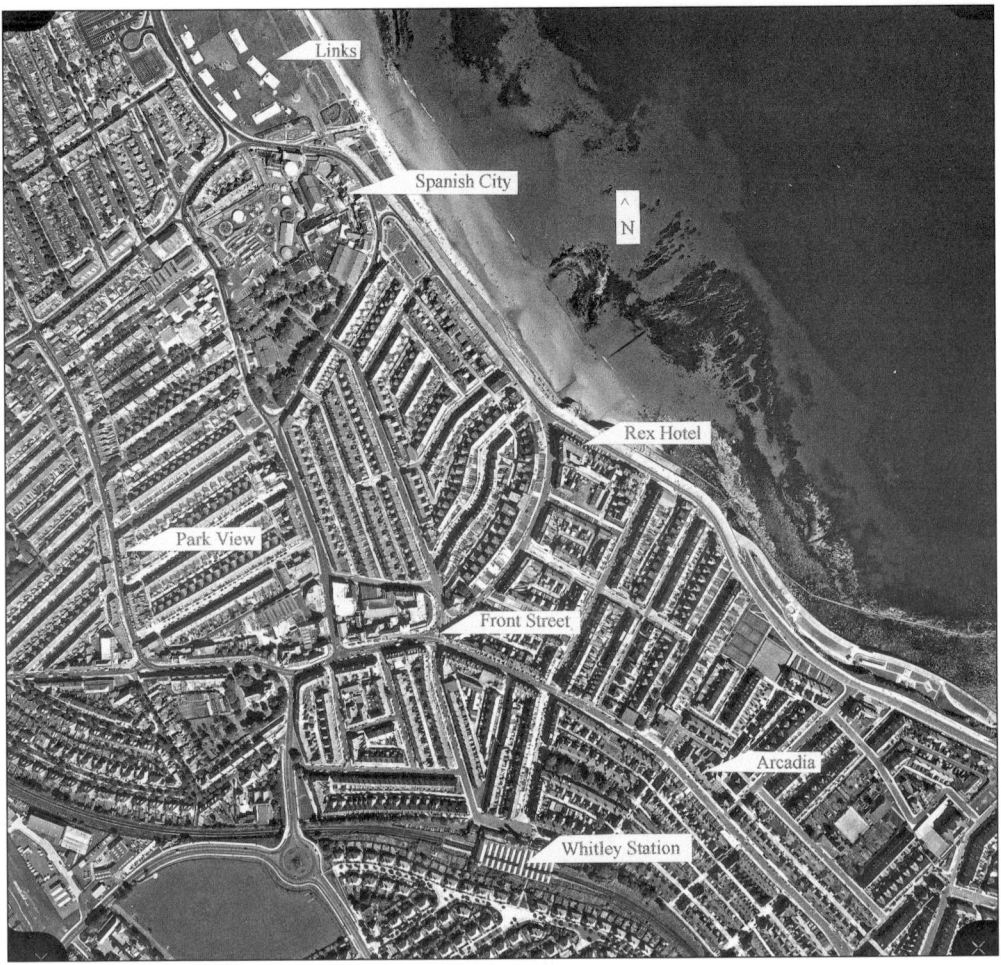

Whitley Bay, 22 August 1974.

Acknowledgements

This book contains a representative sample of the illustrations acquired by North Tyneside Libraries over the last thirty years. To keep to a manageable size and still cover Whitley Bay, regretfully, many pictures had to be left out. For those used, thanks are due to Mrs Armstrong, Mr Bream, F. Brewis, E. Chalmers, D. Cobb, Mrs C. Collier, Mr Cornfoot, Ann Craven, Mr Goonan, Mr A. Hastie, Mr Lingwood, Mrs McKie, Mr Manders, Mr Moffatt, Mr Newton, M. Purdie, Mrs G. Ryan, Mr Scorer, Mr G. Scott, Miss C.E. Smith, A. Senior, Mr Snowdon, W. Taylor, Miss Thompson, A.E. Walton, J.B. West, Mr Whitelock. Some of the most interesting pictures were purchased for the libraries with the help of Mrs Shirley Ellis and Mrs Sheila Ross. Very special thanks are due to Trevor Ermel, of Monochrome, in Newcastle, for last minute reprints. Many members of the public supplied information with the pictures, or volunteered information when they saw a picture in stock. Thanks are due to Mrs Morag Horseman for research, and Mr D. Maddison for his ready fund of memories.

Introduction

In the 1880s Whitley was seen as a 'Dream Village by the Sea'; a suitable home for a few gentlemen. This was long before the name was changed.

Calls for the change began around 1898. In one version of the story, the villagers grew tired of being confused with Whitby. William Oliver of Tynemouth died in Scotland and his body was sent to St Paul's church on 19 September 1901. As a member of many local groups his funeral was well attended, but no coffin arrived. It had in fact been despatched by rail to Whitby and did not arrive at Whitley Station until 8.45 that evening. The burial had to be lamplit. 'Whitley Bay' was the result of local indignation.

The village had come a long way from the tiny hamlet enfeoffed to Tynemouth Priory in 1116. There seems to have been little love lost between the Priors and the de Whitley family. They were the local landholders, and often appear in the Priors' court rolls. One of the earliest references traced relates that in 1225 Ralph de Whitley had failed to provide the 'Conveys'. This was a duty to feed and entertain the Prior, his friends, their servants and animals on the twenty-third and twenty-fourth day of each December.

Gilbert de Whitley had a royal licence to crenellate the tower at his manor house on 9 April 1345. The site had been lost by 1538. After the Dissolution of the Monasteries the estate was divided. Most of the area had been enclosed by 1674, except for the Links.

Early in the eighteenth century John Dove and his brother-in-law Henry Hudson had holdings in the village. Henry Hudson III built Whitley Hall around 1760, the grounds of which took up the south side of the village. His property passed to his niece, Hannah Ellison. She sold the Hall to the Duke of Northumberland in 1817. He also bought the Henzell property on Front Street in 1854. Miss Ellison's executors sold Village Farm to William Davison in 1855. His son, John Thomas Davison, also owned Whitley Dairy Farm, Whitley Lodge Farm and other properties. By 1900 the Duke and Davison's executors were the only large landowners in the township, from Marden Burn in the south-east, to Briardene Burn in the north-west.

Lesser landowners included Henry Trewhitt and Edward Hall. Around 1789 Mr Hall built Whitley Park Hall near the Links. It passed through a number of hands, and was often leased out for summer bathing. In 1857 it was bought by Mr Bulman, who added a wing. He diverted the Blyth road around the grounds, then planted a belt of trees, cutting off his view of the village. He died in 1879 and the Hall remained largely unoccupied until sold to the Whitley Park Hotel Company. Their presence led to the growth of the pleasure gardens later known as Spanish City. Meanwhile, Whitley Hall had failed to find a long-term resident and in 1899 the Duke offered it to the council. They refused, so shops and houses were built on the estate.

The *Whitley Seaside Chronicle* noted that the lack of a single landowner had led to haphazard development since the 1860s, as farmers sold plots here and there. In 1935 Alderman Mason noted that 'squatters fell over each other to make money as land prices rose'. In the 1870s land was being built up in small sections between Front Street and Rockcliffe. Developers included the Alexanders, the Styans, Richard Nesbitt, and James Douglas. John Hilton began the shops on Whitley Road in 1887, and his son carried the new district up to Trewhitt Road in the 1890s. James Hilton and George Robson later added to the section of Whitley Road west of Front Street (Park View). Mr Robson also put up large houses on the seafront, two of which were combined to become the Royal Hotel. Mr Patterson built Brook Street and the Avenue Hotel, opposite Bulman's Hall. A result of all this construction was that in the 1891 census hardly any adults were from Whitley, and many children were born elsewhere. Other major developments included Whitley Links Estate, in 1902, and Grosvenor Estate, in 1904.

By the 1890s there was evident a mix of pride and regret at the speed of the town's growth. A separation between the dormitory town and the health resort showed in the vociferous objection to the building of more hotels in 1899, as it might have depreciated property values.

In the 1870s the only significant buildings on the narrow and dangerous track along the sea banks were Manor House and Whitley Park Terrace. The Local Board of Health first sat in 1874, but was unable to prevent speculative builders working almost to the cliff edge. In 1893 they began the promenade from Rockcliffe to East Parade. It included the Corkscrew Stairs to the beach at the Esplanade. In 1894 they helped free the toll road along the Links. Improvements to the cliff-top road, and the filling of the gully below Park Avenue, continued until 1911, when the Duke of Northumberland performed a formal opening ceremony.

Minor work on the Links culminated with the Northern Lower Promenade in 1914. Central Lower Promenade was begun in 1922, between Watts' Slope and Corkscrew Stairs. The northern section was extended in 1926. The Southern Lower Promenade, from the Esplanade to Table Rocks, opened in 1932.

An Urban District Council first sat in 1895, and soon began the campaign for Incorporation, which came to fruition in 1954. The powers of the Borough and County passed to North Tyneside Council in 1974.

The old village had a farming base, although coal mining was taking place by 1673. In 1684 Henry Hudson had a large limestone quarry at Marden. Through the 1840s the intemperate habits of the colliers gave the district a reputation for drunkenness and violence. When the pit closed in 1848 the population plunged.

Sea bathing began in a small way, but from the 1860s the beach attracted leisure providers. The jewel in the crown of the entertainment trade was the Spanish City, established as Whitley Amusements in 1908. The age of mass tourism had arrived. In the days before cheap continental holidays Whitley Bay was a major resort. Glasgow Fairs Week was the high point of the season. The town was briefly famous for its Lonely Hearts weeks. The loop railway opened up the town and its successor, the Metro, still encourages people across the region to take advantage of Whitley Bay's nightlife.

Recommendations for further reading include *History of Northumberland, volume 8. Parish of Tynemouth*, by H.H.E. Craster (1907); *Historical notes on Cullercoats, Whitley and Monkseaton*, by W.W. Tomlinson (1893); *Blyth & Tyne Railway*, by J.A. Wells (1989); *Spanish City, Whitley Bay: pleasure palace by the sea*, by J. Makepeace (1992). Runs of local newspapers, trades directories, council minutes and censuses are held by the Local Studies Centre of North Tyneside Libraries.

The scope of this compilation is the village, Whitley Road, and the seafront. The library staff would always like to hear from anyone who detects errors or omissions.

One
Up to the Village

Front Street, 1966. Brenda Martin, from the local library, checks the changes since the 1890s. The white-fronted Victoria Hotel is the least altered building. In the intervening period the council offices next door have come and gone.

Arcadia, *c.* 1905. Around 1893 Alfred Styan built these shops on the lane from Cullercoats. To the left, at the northern end, was George Whitehead, a photographer and chemist, who moved to the coast around 1875. Cycleries was run by W.A. Laws. (See page 35.)

Arcadia, *c.* 1910. John Smith took the shop in the centre around 1902, but died in 1903. His widow ran the business into the 1940s. Next door, to the right, was Smurthwaite Bros, the fruiterers. Story's Hardware, to the right, began around 1905.

Trinity Methodist church, 1940. The building, opened in 1889, stood just to the north of Arcadia. On the night of 29 August 1940, it was bombed and burnt out. The health clinic was later built on the site.

Whitley Road, c. 1910. The Station Hotel replaced the post office buildings. From 1900 John Mulholland sought permission to build a hotel on the site, for some time this was opposed on the grounds that the village had all the accommodation it needed.

Whitley Road, *c.* 1910. Although the land south east of the village was being developed for housing as early as the 1860s, Whitley Road was little more than a country lane until the 1890s. Looking back towards Cullercoats, in the distance is Arcadia. To the people of the village the area around the railway station must have looked like a very different type of town. In the summer of 1901 there was a public meeting to protest against turning the old post office buildings at the corner of Whitley Road and Esplanade into a residential hotel. 'It would, if this sort of thing continued, soon mean that the interests of the residents of Whitley would become subservient to those of the casual visitor', was one comment. John Mulholland held the corner as a wine and spirit merchant's until he was able to open the Station Hotel around 1904. Although he had the pub through the 1920s, his occasionally difficult nature led the magistrates in 1922 to renew his licence only if he remained away. The hotel is to the left, on the far side of the street. Station Road is to the right. On the corner the building with a clock was intended, in 1888, to be the Whitley Club Co. A group of gentlemen newly arrived from more populous districts hoped to have a meeting place to rival anything available in the cities. However, the scheme was slow to start, and parts of the premises had to be let out. Around 1895 James Young opened his fashionable draper's store on the ground floor. It became Young & Aiston briefly, then Aiston & Son. This gave way to W.J. Sparkes and around the time of the First World War Lloyd's Bank took over.

Presbyterian church, 31 July 1895. The local congregations have gathered on the Esplanade for the laying of the foundation stone. In the distance is Manor House, standing almost alone on the seafront. The church opened on 23 November 1900.

Esplanade Avenue, c. 1909. The open space between the Esplanade and South Parade began to fill after 1900. The house second from the right was W.H. Woodthorpe's home by 1906. Part of the foreground was built up by 1913.

Linden Terrace, 1915. Robert Elwes, an old-established North Shields draper, moved to this house off the Esplanade around 1913. The picture was possibly taken for his seventy-fifth birthday. He died in 1916, but his daughters continued in residence.

Esplanade, c. 1915. At this time Barclay's Bank was at 39 Esplanade. Next door were Mrs Dawson's bazaar; E. Richley, painter; and Miss F.M. Hately, newsagent. The house with the taller bay was 43 Esplanade, at one time accommodating Beckett-Richley Spiritualists.

Station Road, *c.* 1905. Many trippers must have experienced this as their first view of Whitley Bay on leaving the train. In the distance are Barclay's Bank and the Presbyterian church. To the right is Albany Gardens.

Albany Gardens, 10 August 1916. When a zeppelin cruised over the town on a clear night, the residents rushed out into the streets to watch the searchlights and the single anti-aircraft gun. This improvidence saved their lives.

Station Road, c. 1905. To the left is Aiston and Son's shop. Lloyd's Bank was then next door, and beyond the sign reads 'My Boot Shop'. Presumably this is one of the shops belonging to William Jennings Grummett, renowned as a councillor of decided and disputatious views.

Station Road, c. 1920. The station has been rebuilt and Lloyd's Bank has replaced the draper's, but the Lees are still on the corner to the right. This is during the brief period when Stewart & Lamb occupied 7 Station Road.

16

Whitley Road, 6 July 1893. The parade celebrated the marriage of Prince George and Mary of Teck. It was another two years before much of the street was carried through to the village. The Victoria Hotel is visible in the distance.

Whitley Road, Whitley Bay

Whitley Road, c. 1905. J. Lee was established by the spring of 1904, both as a hairdresser and tobacconist. Ten years earlier the lane had veered round a large pond, near the tram, to enter the village street, glimpsed in the distance.

Whitley Road, *c.* 1907. J. Addison Smith was the first to have shops built between Station Road and the original village, including the Assembly Rooms, to the right. It was run by G. Povesi until 1903.

Whitley Road, *c.* 1905. Alfred Styan built the shops next to the Assembly Rooms in 1895. Mrs Mary Robinson ran her fent shop between 1900 and 1907. She is standing in the doorway to the left with Mary Isabella Davison.

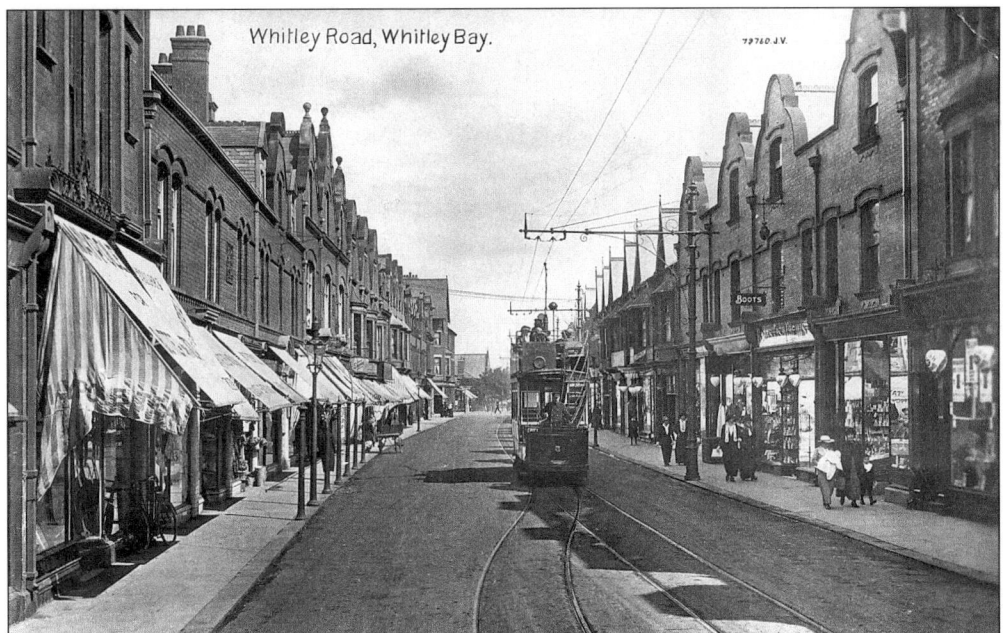

Whitley Road, *c.* 1915. To the left are the blinds of the Maypole Dairy Co., with the Danish Butter shop opposite. Beyond it is Boots Cash Chemists. In the background a handcart stands outside William Taylor's fancy drapery.

Central Buildings, *c.* 1910. The expiration of lease sale at Arthur E. Hogg's shop started on 2 July 1910. Opposite are the Imperial Buildings, with Ellen Darley's confectionery shop on the corner. The entrance to the Central Hall Gospel meetings is on South Parade.

WHITLEY OLD VILLAGE

Front Street, c. 1899. From Charlton's smithy to St Paul's church (hidden by the trees) was the centre of the old Whitley village. To the left is the lodge to Whitley Hall, which stood in its grounds behind the high stone wall. The smithy was the subject of an inquiry in January 1901, as the council wished to buy the workshop from Mrs Pollard. It detracted from the new shops and narrowed the road. Demolition took place later that summer. The workshop had been held by one family since the early 1850s, when Thomas Charlton arrived, possibly from Warden or Haydon Bridge. He married a Monkseaton woman and settled in the cottage next to the workshop. William John Charlton moved to Victoria Terrace, where he kept the business up until his death in 1921. The white building is the Victoria Hotel. It began life around 1832, when John Tinley of North Shields bought an old farm cottage from George Armstrong, and converted it to the Whitley Park Inn. When it was sold in 1838, it was run by William Studdy and the adjoining cottage was leased to Whitley Colliery. Around 1870 it was purchased by James Cowen Landreth, from Berwick, who apparently enlarged the building by incorporating two cottages next door. Certainly the join can still be seen in the photograph. It was possibly his idea to rename the pub as the Victoria Hotel. He retired in the spring of 1888. Shortly afterwards the Victoria can be traced in the hands of Robert Dawson, publican and mineral water manufacturer. Around 1890 he spent £1,000 adding an extra storey and six bedrooms. The hotel was then leased to James Anderson & Co., Newcastle wine and spirit merchants.

Front Street, *c.* 1900. Next door to the Victoria Hotel is a cottage which was demolished to make way for the council offices. They were opened on 1 June 1901 for Whitley and Monkseaton Urban District Council.

Front Street, *c.* 1954. Parts of the council offices were let as shops after 1922. Next door, the cottages were taken down in 1924, and Woolworth's opened on 10 August 1927. In 1955 a larger branch took in both of these sites.

Front Street, c. 1905. To the left is Henry Septimus Proud's fruit shop. In 1901 he moved to the corner with Victoria Terrace, to the left, and lived there until his death in 1911. This, and later Big Lamps, were used as village meeting places.

Front Street, c. 1910. Frank Smith married Isabella Proud in 1904, and in 1907 took over the tobacconist's next door to his father-in-law's fruit shop. He retired in November 1921. The shop became C.H. Brown Ltd.

Front Street, *c.* 1918. The Coliseum Theatre opened behind Whitley House in May 1910. It was extensively altered in 1919, in a cinema conversion, and again in 1929, when it joined the ABC chain.

Front Street, 1952. Next to the New Coliseum is the mock-Tudor frontage added to the Victoria Hotel in 1930. The cinema became Mr Swaddle's bingo hall in the 1960s. To the left is Belvedere House, by this time the pork shop.

Front Street, *c*. 1910. A sign advertises Belvedere House for sale. It was built on the site of John Dove's mansion around 1800, and was the home of the Henzells into the 1850s. In 1915 it was bought for the Belvedere Property Co.

Front Street, 1952. The Belvedere Property Co. acquired Ivy House, at the corner of Park Avenue, and in 1926 built new shops. One of the first traders was Joseph Sampson, a fruiterer, late of Gateshead.

26 Park Avenue, Whitley Bay.

Park Avenue, *c.* 1905. In 1904 the tramlines were extended from Front Street, round past Ivy House (to the right) and Whitley Dairy Farm (in the background). The terminus was moved to the Links. The Ship Inn is to the left (see page 28).

Front Street, *c.* 1890. The trees and wall conceal the grounds of Whitley Hall. The white Ship Inn stands next to Johnson's refreshment rooms, which had been a Wesleyan chapel. St Paul's church dominates the west end of the village.

WHITLEY BAY, THE VILLAGE. Nº3433.

Front Street in 1908. Long after the Whitley Hall grounds were redeveloped for shops and housing, the trees which had stood behind the wall remained. They were cut down in 1922.

Whitley Hall, c. 1894. The Hall faced south, at one time overlooking Whitley Colliery. In 1899 the house and grounds were offered to the Urban District Council, but they refused it, allowing the building up of the south side of Front Street.

St Paul's church, *c.* 1910. The old parish of Tynemouth was divided in 1860 and the Duke of Northumberland provided a new church at the end of Whitley, for the parish of Cullercoats. It was consecrated in 1864.

St Paul's church, *c.* 1911. The interior was remodelled in 1929, when the chancel was cut off by a carved screen. The altar was raised, together with the reredos, and the stone pulpit was replaced with a wooden structure.

Front Street, *c.* 1900. The Ship Inn was rebuilt around 1895, during the residence of Joseph Robinson. Beyond, the houses on Rookery View still have their railed gardens, but were soon to be converted to shops.

Front Street, *c.* 1907. The white building on Rookery View is George Bennion's china shop; earlier a grocery and post office, and later Hately's. To the right is a branch of the North Shields Industrial Society, which opened in November 1902.

Park View, *c.* 1900. The Fat Ox was described as an 'architectural ornament of the district' when it replaced the original in 1869. The shops between the entrance to Northumberland Square and the wall of Steel's market garden were demolished in the 1920s.

Northumberland Square, *c.* 1950. Seen shortly before they were demolished, the local newspaper described the houses as having been one of the most fashionable parts of the village, inhabited by the Duke of Northumberland's personal friends in Victorian days.

Park View, *c.* 1925. In the distance are the shops beside the Fat Ox. Bainbridge & Son, a North Shields firm, opened this furniture shop around 1914. Next door, to the right, is Teesdale's dairy, with Smith's Coronation Coal Depot by the trees.

Park View in 1952. From the mid-1930s there was considerable development on the sites of Steel's garden and the vicarage opposite. Some of the town's more fashionable shops were built here. At the far end of the road the Fat Ox was rebuilt.

Park View, once more in 1952. The early 1930s saw the removal of the old church school from the corner with Norham Road (see page 94). Part of the site was used for the Hotspur dance hall and the associated shops opposite the end of Roxburgh Terrace.

Roxburgh Terrace, c. 1920. St Edward's Roman Catholic church was opened near the Park Avenue corner on 5 March 1911. Next door is St Edward's School, opened in 1914 on part of the old Dairy Farm.

Park Avenue, *c.* 1900. Seen from the stackyard at the end of York Road, Whitley Dairy was then at the northern edge of the old village. In 1925 the post office buildings were put up on part of the farmstead, to the left.

Park Avenue, *c.* 1968. In 1936 the bus station, to the right, replaced the last of the Whitley Dairy. In the distance, E.H. Askew's grocery is on the south side of Front Street.

Public library, 3 January 1940. After thirty years of council opposition, the service opened in rooms over the bus station. Miss Mary Wright was appointed librarian in 1939, and here issues the first book to Councillor W.P. Anderson.

York Road, c. 1967. Elizabeth Coulthard was shortly to move her clothing business to Oxford Street, at the far end of York Road, behind Woolworth's, ahead of a plan to build a supermarket, four shops and a restaurant at this corner.

York Road, *c.* 1900. Seated outside Council Cottage are Mr Mather and Thomas Thompson, with Mr Moore, the Urban District Surveyor. Robert James Wilkin, hackmaster, is in the doorway to the right. The cottage was behind the council offices on Front Street.

York Road, *c.* 1910. Council Cottage was demolished to allow Northumberland Constabulary to build a fire station. In those days the police also provided the fire and ambulance services. The building, equipped with stables and family flats, opened on 8 May 1909.

South Parade, *c.* 1910. Opposite the end of York Road, W.A. Laws converted a house into the Exchange Buildings. The opening ceremony was held on 11 June 1910, with entertainment provided by the newly formed Whitley Bay Military Band.

North Parade, *c.* 1895. Whitley Cottages was the home of Thomas Robson, cowman. North Parade followed the cattle path to a well. William Crawford, one-time secretary of the Miners' National Association, is said to have been born here in 1883.

Oxford Street, *c.* 1905. After several years using a tin chapel, the Primitive Methodist church opened on the site of Whitley Cottages on 17 March 1904. To the left is Oxford Street, leading northwards to Whitley Park Hall.

Ocean View, 16 April 1941. Two landmines were dropped between Oxford Street and the promenade, bracketing Ocean View. There was considerable loss of life among the service personnel billeted there, although a canary was found alive and singing in the rubble.

Two

Transport

RAILWAY STATION WHITLEY BAY

Whitley Station, c. 1905. In the days before widespread private transport many tourists and residents alike used the railway to travel to Whitley Bay. In this, the 1882 station, the only entrance was on the north side, to the right, which was inconvenient for the growing volume of traffic.

Station Road. Whitley Bay. (749)

Station Road, *c.* 1913. The Blyth & Tyne Railway Company built a track past Whitley village, to its terminus at Tynemouth Road, Tynemouth, in 1864. The line was further inland than the present Metro route, and the nearest station to the village was at Hillheads. The first Whitley Station was at the site of Souter Park, to the chagrin of the inhabitants of Monkseaton, which was then the larger village. In 1874 the North Eastern Railway Co. took over the Blyth & Tyne Railway. Plans were laid for the North Tyne Loop, including a track closer to the coast and its expanding villages. This necessitated replacing the Whitley Station at Monkseaton with one on the present site. The new line opened in 1882, although a newspaper noted, 'We are given to understand that had the Company not been able to utilise the roofing material of the old Blyth & Tyne and North Eastern Stations at Tynemouth, the people of Whitley and Cullercoats would not have had such handsome structures erected for their convenience and pleasure as the new stations are'. In 1889 Thomas Harvey, station master at Whitley, was presented with a biscuit box, as a prize for his garden, and 'the refining influence it must have had on all classes of society'. As late as 1969 the station was still winning prizes for its decorations. To deal with complaints about the convenience of the station, North Eastern Railway prepared plans for new buildings in 1908. The larger station, with its clock tower, was built in 1910. In 1920 there was a presentation to Mr A. Whitehorn, clerk to the council. 'The phenomenal development and increase in population during the last 43 years' were credited to his negotiations for a station.

Bandstand terminus, *c.* 1914. Tynemouth & North Shields District Tramway Co. used horses to try the line to Front Street at the beginning of 1901. The electric service began in March and was extended to the Links in 1904.

Bandstand terminus, *c.* 1925. The trams ran between North Shields and Whitley Bay until 4 August 1931. Towards the end, however, they had been alternating with buses. The council pulled up the tramroad and used the sets to build banks in the seafront gardens.

Spanish City, *c.* 1913. The blackboard next to the bus advertises the running of the Favourite Service – to Hartley, Blyth, Seaton Delaval, and along the coast. The Favourite was operated by George Metcalfe, whose Whitley Motor Co. established a large garage on Marden Road, next to St Paul's church, around 1913.

North Eastern Railway bus, *c.* 1914. The company acquired a fleet of Fiat charabancs in 1907, running service routes and tours of the district.

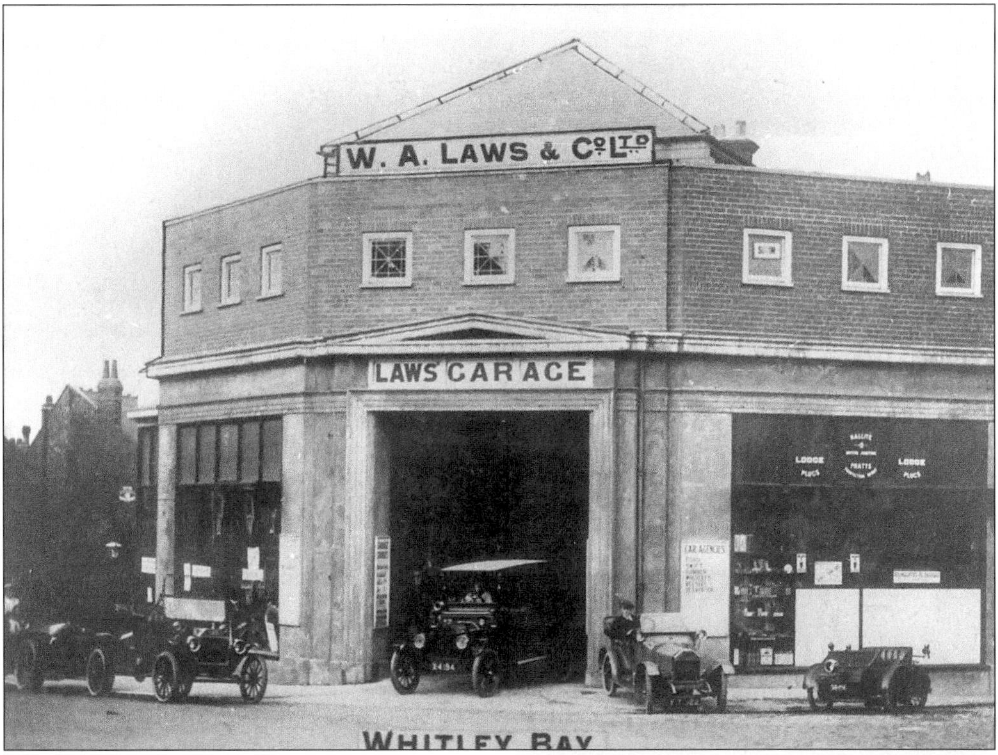

Oxford Street, *c.* 1914. W.A. Laws' garage opened between Exchange Buildings and the Primitive Methodist church in the spring of 1914, with Ford, Detroiter, and Swift car agencies. It was run by Herbert Laws.

Elizabeth Shiels, *c.* 1916. In 1897 the *Whitley Seaside Chronicle* noted, 'Scores of occupations that but a few years ago the most optimistic of ladies would never have dreamed of seeing placed at the disposal of their sex, are now gladly held open for them.' Even so, it took a war to bring a chauffeuse to Laws' garage.

41

Taxi, c. 1910. William Thompson drove this car for the Waverley Hotel. Provided by Wakefield of North Shields, it is believed to be have been the first taxi to operate in Whitley Bay.

Whitley Dairy, c. 1905. Down the years parking has proved a particular source of irritation to the people of Whitley Bay. How much simpler when you could just leave your transport at Hickey's Dairy and get onto a tram.

Thomas Dunn, *c.* 1910. Small two-wheeled delivery carts once thronged the streets. Thomas Dunn opened his fish, game and poultry shop at Duke Street in 1898. This is one of his sons, also Thomas, who had the shop at Monkseaton.

Pantechnicon, *c.* 1910. Bainbridge & Son were an old-established North Shields auction house, who opened a branch in Whitley Road, near Boots, around 1900. Later they had furniture showrooms on Park View. (See page 30.)

Empress, c. 1930. The Frys of Tynemouth had been boat builders and operators since the eighteenth century. Their *Empress* is loading passengers from wheeled gangways on the beach at Whitley, below the central promenade, while *Majestic* stands off.

Slipway men, *c.* 1950. The trips to St Mary's Island required considerable labour on the mobile landing stages

Three
The Links

Links, *c.* 1914. To the north of Whitley Park Terrace is the slope to Watts' Café and the helter-skelter. Beyond, the grassy banks stretch up to St Mary's Island. The sign instructs motor vehicles and cycles to keep to a walking pace along the promenade.

Links, *c.* 1913. Children cluster round the drinking fountain outside Smith's Café. In the background are the bandstand and the tower of the Prudhoe Home, whose windmill pump for seawater baths is to the right. Most of the housing will be built twenty years in the future.

Links, *c.* 1935. The sunken gardens were constructed by the council in 1933, to provide an area slightly shaded from the winds off the sea. At the bandstand is the marquee for the Super Entertainers, a concert party popular in the 1930s.

Cenotaph, 1922. To commemorate the dead of the First World War, the council laid the foundation stone of the cenotaph on 1 October 1921. It was unveiled by the Duke of Northumberland on 15 July 1922.

Links, c. 1905. The Links a little earlier had been occupied by Jeremiah Nicholson's brickworks, which was sold in April 1904. A few houses, as far as the site of Eastbourne Gardens, can be seen in the foreground. In the distance are the Prudhoe Memorial Convalescent Home and Whitley Park Farm.

Panama Café, *c.* 1900. Whitley Links were almost the last unenclosed part of the old Shire Moor. In the 1800s the heughs were hummocky with the spoil of coal and ironstone mines, and covered with gorse. The golf club, founded in 1890, is credited with clearing the thickets and levelling the ground. In the dip is Panama House, a café built by Stephen Fry, around 1895, possibly replacing an earlier tea-room. He had been a diver on the Panama Canal and one version of the story has it that the central building came from the wrecked *Panama*. The interior was fitted up to give a shipboard feel. After Stephen Fry's death in 1912 the building was bought by the council and leased to William Laidlow. He died in 1941, shortly after war-time restrictions closed the café. 'Residents of Whitley Bay stood on the Links looking down into the hollow where the Panama Café was ablaze last night', wrote the *Shields Evening News* on 13 March 1945. After the war the council built a new Panama Café on the Northern Promenade. In 1890 a formal document for tenancy of the Links was drawn up between the Local Board of Health and the Duke of Northumberland. Stintholders had a right to graze from 13 May to 11 November each year. In Victorian times various Volunteer Corps camped on the Links; rifle and artillery practice was common. According to Edward Elliott of Earsdon:

> The great round shot went plish for plash
> Into the tortured deep,
> They myed the crabs an' lobsters hop,
> An' the fish could get nee sleep.

Stephen Fry. The Frys had been involved in the tourist industry for a century when Stephen Fry built Panama House. Standing well over six feet, and with a supply of tall tales to match, he became one of the tourist features of Whitley.

Panama Dip, c. 1938. The gardens and a bandstand were planned in 1933. The glass windscreens were added in 1935. This bandstand was replaced with a fountain in memory of Doris Ewbank and other Civil Defence personnel killed in the Second World War.

Prudhoe Memorial Convalescent Home, *c.* 1910. As a memorial to the fourth Duke of Northumberland, this building was opened by public subscription on 14 September 1869. The Home operated in conjunction with the Newcastle Infirmary and the Convalescent Society of Northumberland and Durham. They provided beds for sixty-five males and twenty-five females. Subscribers to the charity were entitled to nominate the deserving poor for places in the Home. In 1959 Whitley Borough Council bought the building and on 1 April 1974 the Leisure Pool opened on the site.

Prudhoe Home in 1936.

Links, *c.* 1914. The house with the white verandah was known as Whitley Villa, or Link House. This was, from around 1880, the home of Ernst Emil Biesterfield, shipbroker and Greek vice-consul. It stood near the present St Mary's Avenue. In the background are some of the many chalets, caravans and tents condemned and demolished by the council in 1929.

BRIAR DENE HOTEL

Briar Dene Hotel, *c.* 1904. Previously the Culvert Inn, it stood next to a bridge over a narrow dene. A toll was imposed between 18 June 1840 and 2 May 1894, when, acting on behalf of the local authorities, Sir Matthew White Ridley kicked down the gate.

Links in 1952. The old lane to Seaton Sluice and Blyth has been replaced by a dual carriageway. In the distance are the cemetery, begun in 1913, and the holiday park next door.

Caravan site, c. 1955. Caravans had been a regular sight along the Links since the early part of the century, especially just north of the Prudhoe Home. Around 1964 discussions over a park at the Hartley Army Camp began, leading eventually to the opening of the Feathers site in the summer of 1965.

St Mary's Island, *c.* 1890. Otherwise known as Bates Island, or Hartley Bates, by tradition it had a chapel dedicated to St Mary by a Prior of Tynemouth Abbey. It is said to have contained a light to guide wrecked mariners and a bell to summon help. The first record of anyone actually living on the island dates from the late 1850s, when George Ewen took a twelve year lease, with the right to build a hut to store his salmon nets. The island was part of Hartley East Farm, owned by Lord Hastings. The Salmon Fisheries Act of 1861 damaged Mr Ewen's fishing potential, so he obtained a beer license and opened the Square and Compass Inn. In 1885 estate workers were provided, free of charge, to help him build a long room at the pub. Customers came from as far away as Bedlington on Sundays. This led to friction with the farmer, Mr Pattison, who objected to having his fields trampled and his fences broken. The police began to object to the license, claiming that the pub was difficult to supervise. Allegedly on the advice of his friends among the miners, John Ewen claimed squatters rights to St Mary's Island, as a result of which he was served with notice to quit. After a court case, the Ewens were evicted from the estate in November 1895. On the 31 August 1896 John Livingstone Miller began work on the foundations of a new Trinity House lighthouse. The lighthouse was first lit in September of 1898, replacing a light which had stood at Tynemouth Priory since the eighteenth century. At first the light was oil-fuelled, but an automatic lamp was introduced in 1977. The light was decommissioned in 1984, and in 1986 North Tyneside Council acquired the buildings for use as a visitors centre.

John Ewen in November 1895. The family had all their goods, even down to the inn sign, deposited on the Links. They are presumably surrounded by the mourning customers.

St Mary's Lighthouse, *c.* 1898. Stanley Miller, a son of the contractor, was the foreman on the job. He went on to found an international construction company.

St Mary's Island, *c.* 1930. At low tide it is possible to cross the causeway to the island. In the past a boat trip from the beach further south was an alternative.

Gothenburg City in 1891. The ship, carrying cattle and timber, came ashore on St Mary's Island in a fog on 26 June. Although the cargo and crew were rescued, not all the efforts of the tugs could shift her from the rocks. For a time she became something of a tourist attraction.

St Mary's Island Camp, *c.* 1916. During both World Wars the seafront at Whitley Bay was heavily occupied by the armed services. These are Royal Army Medical Corps and Royal Artillerymen at the canteen.

Links, *c.* 1918. Captured Germans were held in a camp at Whitley. In 1919 Dr Frederick Horseman, a spiritualist and a committed Christian, was arrested for 'a very serious offence'. The war being over, he had seen no objection to giving the prisoners of war a box of apples. (See page 91.)

Northern Lower Promenade, *c.* 1955. Looking south towards the dome at the Spanish City there is an open space on the terracing behind the promenade, where the beach chalets used to stand.

THE CHALETS, LOWER PROMENADE WHITLEY BAY. 13438

Northern Lower Promenade, *c.* 1938. In June 1936, twenty-five chalets were built by Mr Kirsop and were sold to the council in the same year. In September 1940 they were requisitioned. It was not until 1959 that twenty-five new chalets were built. They remained standing until 1990.

Northern Lower Promenade in 1938. From the Panama Bathing Station, opened 18 June 1938, it is possible to see in the distance the line of chalets on their rotating bases. The council rented them to people who wanted a base down by the sea; it was, however, forbidden to live in them. From 1907 the council had been laying paths on the Links and constructing various minor works. Councillor Dowling was later to claim that a visit to Bournemouth in 1908 gave him the idea for the lower promenade. Several suggestions were put forward, and rejected on the grounds of cost. A series of plans were adopted, and the first stage of the Northern Lower Promenade was opened by the Lord Mayor of Newcastle in June 1914. In that year the council took over the hire of the beach's 1,200 deckchairs, and soon found them insufficient to meet the demand. The promenade was extended northwards from Panama Dip in 1926, and a new café opened in 1930. Rendevous Café was inaugurated in 1949. The Panama Swimming Club opened their pavilion on 5 July 1931. At the outbreak of the Second World War the military authorities closed the beach. Their trip lines and barbed wire remained long after VE Day.

Panama House, c. 1914. This appears to be lunch for a whole coach trip. Surely the price is wishful thinking?

Panama Dip, c. 1913. In the distance is the dome of the Empress Theatre at the Spanish City, which opened in 1910. Below and to the right is part of the verandah surrounding Panama House.

Northern Lower Promenade, *c.* 1914. The wide promenade, with the terracing and stairs down from the shelters on the Links, was formally opened in June 1914.

Hunter's donkeys, *c.* 1905. Rides along the sands were an essential part of the holiday experience. Mr Hunter was one of the early donkey keepers. Joseph Lawson instigated the Donkey Derbies which were run during Race Week between the World Wars.

The Sands, Whitley Bay.

Watts' Café, *c.* 1910. Andrew
Hodgson Watts had a café in North
Shields before he came to Whitley
to build. His granddaughters,
Elizabeth Jane and Mary Ann, ran
the café for many years.

Steve Watts, *c.* 1935. Another
grandchild of A.H. Watts, Steve
came to Whitley in 1880. Later he
was the owner of some twenty
rowing boats, which were hired from
the beach. He retired in 1947 and
died in 1950.

Helter-skelter, *c.* 1907. This slide was usually erected close to Watts' Café.

Four
Entertainers and Sports

LEON DODD'S "SUPER ENTERTAINERS" (1933)
LINKS BANDSTAND PAVILION   WHITLEY BAY...

Super Entertainers in 1933. Pierrots, or concert parties, were a major attraction in seaside resorts, frequently playing in the open air or under canvas.

Toreadors, *c.* 1905. In 1904 part of the Whitley Park Hall estate was being used as a playing field by the Rockcliffe Rugby Football Club, when Charles Elderton of Hebburn brought his concert party there to play summer season on a temporary stage. The Toreadors became a popular part of the summer scene and Whitley Amusements began to build up a fairground around them, starting with booths painted with Spanish themes – hence Spanish City. Whitley Amusements was taken over by the Whitley Pleasure Gardens Company Ltd in 1909. The latter firm founded the Empress Theatre, which opened in 1910. Charles Elderton and H. Fail were the new company's managing directors. From June to September 1910 the Toreadors played at a new venue, the Summer Gardens, Whitley Promenade. They had a stage and covered seating area on what later became the bowling green at Victoria Park. The company seems to have split up afterwards, because in the next year Charles Elderton was presenting Elderton's Entertainers, and by the beginning of the First World War he was running the Hello Minstrels. Many other concert parties played short dates on the Links bandstand and elsewhere. In 1914 the Debonairres built the Kursaal on Park Road, which eventually became the Playhouse. Leon Dodd appeared at the bandstand and the open air theatre on the Central Lower Promenade. His obituary in 1954 notes that he first brought a minstrel show to Whitley Bay in 1929, and that he played the bandstand every year until 1939. The troupe included his wife, Bunty Gordon, and daughter Fay Lenore. In the winter he toured in pantomime.

Busy Bees, 1925. This was the resident group at the bandstand for the summer of 1925. By tradition concert parties played the first half of the show in pierrot costume, before changing to formal dress.

Catlin's Royal Pierrots in 1908. W. Catlin began his career on the promenade around 1904. He made repeated applications to build a Kursaal at Brook Street, but it fell to one of the players, Walter Amner, with Will Houghton, to succeed.

Super Entertainers in 1934. Leon Dodd is seated in the centre. The girls kneeling to either side of him are Minzi and Mena, who continued to play at the Station Hotel into the 1970s. Behind him is John Armstrong. Bunty Gordon is standing second from the left.

Whitley, Monkseaton and District Amateur Operatic Society, c. 1928. The area has supported a variety of active amateur performers. This is a scene from *The Arcadians*, on stage at the Empress.

Thomas Dunn's cart, *c.* 1910. Presumably decorated for one of the horse parades or a carnival, in daily life the cart would have delivered fish. The girl is Doris Dunn, with her brothers Stanley and Peter. Thomas junior is holding the pony.

Whitley Road in 1924. The parade is passing Barclays Bank, at the Esplanade. The carnivals were a major feature of the summers during the 1920s. The town also held Busking Days for charity.

Cullercoats fishwife Polly Donkin and blind concertina player Martin Henderson. He orginated Busking Day for Newcastle Infirmary, and she collected for the lifeboats.

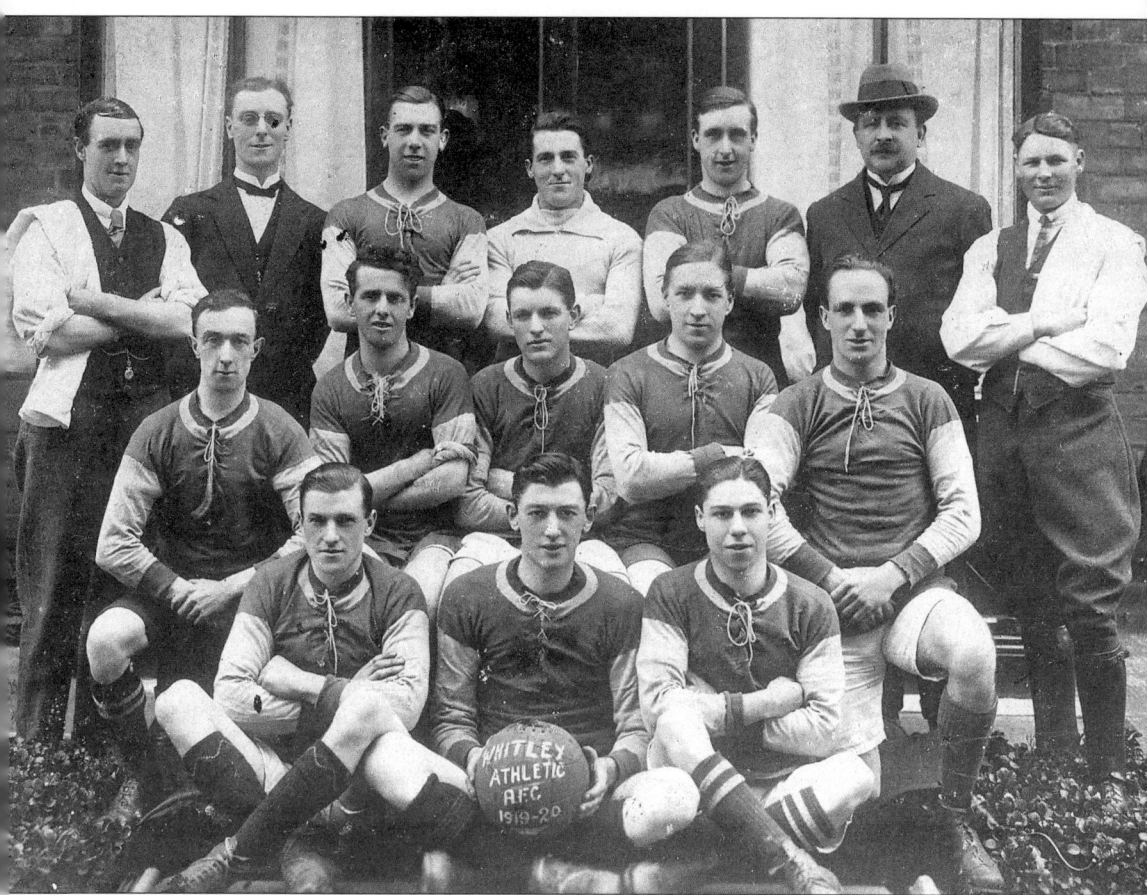

Whitley Athletic, 1919/20. The area supported a wide range of sporting activities, although they were strangely under-reported in the local press. This was probably caused by the expectation that club secretaries would send in details rather than the newspaper seeking them. Whitley Athletic acquired a ground at Marden Road in 1914, when they played in the Northern Amateur League and Charity Cup competitions and for the Northumberland Amateur Cup. In the 1920s and 1930s they were part of the Whitley and District League, along with Belvedere United, Monkseaton Celtic, Monkseaton Rangers, Old Seatonians, St John's Wesleyans, Whitley and Monkseaton Methodists, Whitley Congos, Whitley IGOT, Whitley Rovers, 1st and 2nd Whitley Scouts. Whitley Welfare AFC began in 1933. Rockcliffe Rugby Club was founded in 1887, and regularly won the County Cup. The golf club, founded in 1890, moved from the Links to Nicholson's Farm in 1906. Whitley Cycling Club was one of the oldest in the county; later the Rockcliffe Wheelers were founded. At least two swimming clubs patronised the Table Rocks pool. There were cricket and hockey teams, and quoits was an old favourite. On 8 May 1914 the old Assembly Rooms became Whitley Sports Club, with 200 members. (See page 18.)

Whitley Wednesday, c. 1910. From left to right, standing: J. Hilton (president), J. Lamb, J.V. Wedderburn, W. Palmer (secretary), A. Dawson, G. Smith, J. Gardner, R. Brown, G. Routledge, J. Swales, T. Swalwell, J. Thompson, W. Coverdale, J. Taylor. Seated: T. Lamb, G. Harrison, T. Sellars, W. Winter. On the ground: J. Elgey, W. Attridge, T. Crocker (captain), G. Dobson, J. Sellars. The small boy is unknown.

Whitley Celtic, 1921/22. Celtic played in the Whitley and District Junior League. The goalkeeper is Robert Gay, whose father was a draper in the town. He also played for Whitley Amateurs.

Whitley and Monkseaton Amateur FC, *c.* 1936. From left to right, on the back row, are: J. Thompson, J. Dunn, J. Nicholson, W. Doxford, T. Joyce, R. Belshaw. On the front row are: C. Reid, R. Laverick, A. Bolton, W. Kennedy, P. McCreadie. They were third in the Northern Alliance and finalists in the Tynemouth Infirmary Cup on 27 April 1936.

Victoria Park in 1954. The bowling green on the promenade near Rockcliffe, where Charles Elderton once erected the Summer Gardens under canvas.

Walking race, 29 July 1903. The boys raced to Holywell Dene and back, but the main event was the men's race to Earsdon, Seaton Sluice and back to the council offices via Hartley. The youngest contestant was J. Bolam, age 10.

Links, 11 August 1907. Due to the weather being fine there was a large attendance at the Whitley Cycling Club Church Parade. This bandstand was removed to the new gardens at Rockcliffe in 1908.

Five
Spanish City

Spanish City in the 1950s. The Virginia Reel and the Figure 8 Railway dominate the fairground. To the bottom left is the Playhouse. The council offices are in the long, low buildings to the right.

WHITLEY BAY FROM THE AIR (2000 FEET UP) A. B4848.

Spanish City, *c*. 1922. Even between the World Wars there were open spaces in the heart of the town. The areas around Coquet Avenue and Eastbourne Gardens appear to be laid out as allotments. In the centre, the area between the promenade and Park Road comprises the grounds of the former Whitley Park Hall. The Hall itself, dating from the 1700s, can be seen at the edge of the trees on the extreme left. Towards the end of the last century it became the Park Hotel and the grounds began to be developed for entertainment purposes, culminating in the Spanish City. Below the Hall are two long single storey buildings, said to have been used as RNAS aircraft hangars on the Links during the First World War. After the war they were rebuilt on this site by the Priory Catering Co., and run as a dance hall and skating rink. In 1922 the council bought the old Hall for use as offices but it proved unsatisfactory, so they moved into the Priory Catering Co. premises as a temporary measure. They remained there for sixty years. Princess Café is in the centre of Whitley Park Terrace, with the Empress Ballroom to the right. It opened as a theatre and centrepiece of the Spanish City in 1910. Opposite Watts' Slope, to the bottom right, is the Pavilion Electric Theatre, which opened in 1910 and burned down in 1923. On the site of the Playhouse is the Kursaal, opened by the Debonairres Concert Party in 1913. Marine Avenue runs up to Monkseaton in the background.

74

Links, *c.* 1906. Whitley Park Terrace and Grice's baths are to the right, beyond Smith's Café. There are lots of wide open spaces along the promenade, most notably at the Pleasure Gardens.

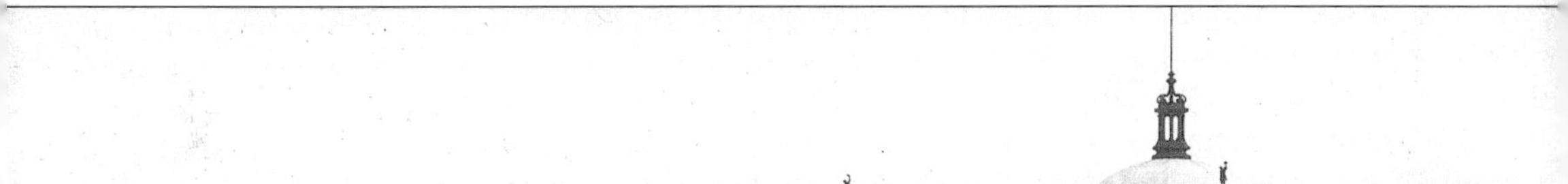

Links, *c.* 1912. Smith's cabin is still on the promenade, but now the Empress Theatre has been built, the baths have become a cinema and there are public shelters in the Brook Street gardens.

Watts' Slope, *c.* 1914. Robert Smith was a Scotsman, who applied to open his cocoa rooms in April 1890. At the time the promenade had not been built and the café was on a grassy bank above Watts' Slope.

Spanish City, 9 July 1924. Beyond the Cenotaph is the burned out shell of the Pavilion Electric Theatre. "Answers", a popular magazine was holding a Gala Day at the Spanish City.

Spanish City, 1910. In the spring G. Mouchel & Partners of Westminster, took a set of photographs of their latest project. They had designed these ferro-concrete cantilevers. The architects were James T. Cackett and R. Burns Dick, and the contractors were Hennebique concrete specialists Samuel F. Davidson & Miller. The 1,400 seat theatre, with a gallery for 400, a roof garden and promenade, opened on 4 May 1910. A few days previously the structure had been tested with sandbags and 150 workmen who were set to marching up and down.

Spanish City, 1910. Close examination reveals workmen putting the final touches to the Empress and its shops. The large box by the main door advertises the imminent opening.

Spanish City, *c.* 1912. Apparently the two little girls pursued the photographer Burton Graham until he took their picture. They were Emily Brough, born 1908, and Millicent Brough, born 1901, of Duchess Street.

Pavilion Electric Theatre, *c.* 1910. In 1897 Robert L. Grice built his Sea Water Baths Pavilion on Whitley Park Terrace. Within a few years he was using the Pavilion for putting on entertainment – variety turns during the week and choral concerts on Sundays. The Pavilion began to show films in 1909, and in 1910 became the first full time cinema in Whitley Bay. Early in the morning of 20 December 1923, the building was discovered to be on fire. It could not be saved.

Spanish City, *c.* 1924. To the right is the entrance to the Picture House, with posters for *The Avalanche* and *Six Days*, by Elinor Glyn.

Spanish City, *c.* 1929. The Picture House was founded by Richard W. Brown, one of the earliest film exhibitors on Tyneside. In July 1916 he was running the Pavilion Electric Theatre and announced that he intended to open a new picture hall at the Spanish City. The Picture House closed in 1963.

David Ross, *c.* 1920. On each side of the Picture House David Ross had shops selling fancy goods. He continued to trade well into the 1960s. His parents sold drinks and ices inside the rotunda.

Whitley Park Terrace, *c.* 1925. Mark Hewitt was a dairyman at Chirton Lane Farm. In the 1920s he had shops next to the cinemas at the Spanish City. After the fire at the Pavilion, this frontage was widened.

Empress Ballroom in 1926. The posters note the newly introduced Sunday café concerts; Whitley Bay was 'going Continental'. Among the staff, third from the left is Harry Hall, handyman and boilerman, to his left is Mr Spence, the manager.

Empress Ballroom in 1920. The old Empress Theatre was converted to a ballroom decorated in cream and gold, with silvered panels on the walls and balcony. The main floor could take 750 dancers, with a further 150 in a side hall.

Charter Day, 14 April 1954. Local government in Whitley had passed from the parish to the Local Board, and then to the Urban District Council. Since the turn of the century they had campaigned for Borough status. Some services were provided by Northumberland County Council and the town was reliant on other authorities for electricity and water. Eventually years of planning and petitioning paid off and the Charter was signed in March 1954. Here the Princess Royal and the Charter Mayor, Councillor Roger M. Charlton, are seated on the stage of the Empress Ballroom for the formal handing over ceremony. The town clerk, A.S. Ruddock, is reading the address of welcome. Seated on the right is the Revd F.R. Hedley, vicar of St Paul's church.

Spanish City, *c.* 1910. The newly constructed Water Chute replaced the Social Whirl. The residents of Elmwood Terrace, to the left, had objected to its noise.

Water Chute, *c.* 1910. In the background are a few remnants of the Spanish scenes on canvas awnings, which gave the pleasure gardens their name. In the distance is Marine Avenue, before development.

Rainbow Pleasure Wheel, *c.* 1913. A company was set up to import this device from the United States. It was completed in June 1914 and thousands rode around at up to 40mph. It was hailed as a success, but seems not to have lasted long.

Virginia Reel, c. 1925. Just as the Social Whirl had given way to the Water Chute, so it in turn was replaced by this larger version of the original attraction. It survived into the 1950s.

Social Whirl, *c.* 1910. Nichol Ritchie's complaints of the intrusive nature of this ride caused a team of American fairground engineers to jack up the whole ride and move it in one piece to the opposite side of the site.

Great Aerial Flight, *c.* 1920. Pylon rides were popular at the time. As it rotated the gondolas lifted away from the vertical. In the background is Whitley Park Hall.

Figure 8 Railway, *c.* 1911. The ride opened on Easter Monday, 12 April 1909 and lasted until early in 1974. In the background is one of the earliest attractions – Ye Old Mill. It carried customers past scenes from Fairyland.

Spanish City, *c.* 1912. The Old Mill ride has been converted to offer an experience of the South Pole. This was the year of the Scott expedition to Antarctica.

The House That Jack Built, *c.* 1910. This was another of the original attractions in the pleasure gardens. In the distance are the houses at the foot of Park Avenue.

The House That Jack Built, *c.* 1914. Close inspection shows that it was not always the same structure.

Avenue Hotel, *c.* 1914. The hotel, built by Thomas Patterson, opened on 24 June 1907. The proprietress was Mrs Mary Alice Morgan, who also ran the Whitehall next door, on the left.

Priory House, *c.* 1893. Annie Philipson conceived of Priory House as a convalescent home for the sick poor, and decided to build and run it at her own expense. It opened at the foot of Park Avenue, in front of Park Hall, on 9 February 1893.

Park Road, *c.* 1939. Built in the late eighteenth century, Whitley Park Hall was the home of Edward Hall. After his death in 1792 the Hall was sold to Thomas Wright, who died in 1840. The *Tyne Pilot* newspaper noted in 1842 that the Blyth to North Shields stagecoach passed the empty building twice a day. They suggested that the house would make an excellent hotel for sea bathers. It was certainly leased out during the summer months. It may have been to avoid the stagecoach that Mr Bulman had the road diverted, after he bought the Hall in 1857. He also planted the belt of trees, which screened the enlarged grounds. After he died in 1879 the Hall remained largely unoccupied until sold to the Whitley Park Hotel Company. Their presence encouraged the growth of the pleasure gardens later known as Spanish City. During the First World War the house was requisitioned by the Army. Amid much controversy in 1922 the Urban District Council acquired the property, intending to convert it for use as new council offices. Unfortunately, the premises had deteriorated to such an extent that they were not fully usable. In July 1939 Mr J.C. Boomer wrote to the council complaining that the contract for demolishing the council offices in the park had proved very disappointing. It had taken longer than expected, and involved him in heavy labour costs. They voted to give him another £50. The grounds had been laid out as a public park, and between the World Wars there were regular programmes of band concerts.

Park bandstand, c. 1930.

Whitley and Monkseaton councillors, c. 1937. From left to right, standing at the back: -?-, -?-, W.P. Anderson, B. Fender, W. King, N. Richley, C. Crisp, -?-, Dr Horseman. Middle row: -?- (policeman), J. Thompson, J.H. Grant (?), G.H. Mayhew, A.J. Rousell, Dr W. Cunningham, J.H. Strachan, G.D.J. Leinster, R.M. Charlton, -?-, G. Henderson, G. Holden, -?- (policeman). Seated: M.M. Snowball, -?-, J.R. Coates, W. Fairhurst (?), A.J. Napp, G. Wilkinson, Mrs Laws, -?-, -?-, R. Madgen, -?-, S. Pearson, -?-.

Library, 6 October 1966. Standing in for Dame Irene Ward, Mayor of Whitley Bay, Alderman J.H. Baglee is speaking at the official opening of the new library in the park. Seated, centre, is the librarian, Miss Mary Wright.

Library in 1966. The council decided to leave the bus station premises when the provision of library services became compulsory. The Waring & Netts building, almost on the site of the old Park Hall, opened on 15 August 1966.

Six

Schools

St Paul's School in 1909. The building at the corner of Norham and Whitley Roads was a Church of England school. The teacher to the right is known to be Miss Thompson. The first girl on the left, in the second row back, is Bertha Barber. Elizabeth Barber is second from the right on the front row.

National School in 1932. A signboard on the corner reads 'This land available for immediate development, Temple & Pyle Ltd, contractors', which places the date between 1930 and 1932. The National Society for Promoting the Education of the Poor in the Principles of the Established Church was active long before education became compulsory. The National Schools Movement believed that the working classes of the manufacturing districts would be only too happy for their children to be instructed by local clergy. They would see their children daily become more orderly, cleanly, industrious and in all respects better members of the domestic circle. At Whitley village the newly formed parish of Cullercoats induced the Duke of Northumberland to donate a site at the corner of what became Norham Road and Park View. The school was built at the expense of Mrs Abbott of Beaufront Castle, near Hexham. It opened in 1871 with space for 236 children. Even after the 1870 Education Act, the village had no Board School, and St Paul's continued when the Urban District became responsible for education in 1902. Within a few years the North and South Council Schools opened. Northumberland County Council built the secondary school just outside the village in 1914. Other schools known to have been in the area include Gordon College, Miss Hawden's, Mallinson and Pringle's, the Mount Preparatory School, Miss Taylor's, Lancelot Geo. W. Wilkinson's, and the Whitley and Monkseaton Business Training College, run by Miss Edna McIntosh at Eastcliffe. In more recent times the council acquired St Mary's Lighthouse, partly as an aid to teaching children about the environment.

Park School, *c.* 1905. This is North Council School, seen from what became the back garden of 9 Coquet Avenue. It opened in 1905 with room for 1,020 pupils. This was the infants' section, and later housed Coquet Park First School.

Park School, *c.* 1906. Immediately behind the two boys lying down is Aynesley Newton.

Tynemouth Municipal High School, 27 January 1912. The teaching unit at St Mary's Lighthouse was not a totally new idea. This group was on a nature walk from Briar Dene to the island.

Rockcliffe School class in 1911. The teacher is Miss Hilda Robson.

Rockcliffe School, in 1911. South Council School was officially opened on 10 May 1911. The head teachers were Mr Turnbull and Miss Brown.

Rockcliffe School, c. 1968. From left to right, back row: Anthony Barber, John Eggdale, Gary Heslop, Mark ?, Wendy Fleck, Lisa Riach, Janie Dutton, Makon Seeborn, Tommy Robson, Mark Charlton, Linda Frazer. Middle row: Susan Dougherty, Neil Brown, -?-, possibly Michell Henderson, Gareth Marshall, Tina Lamb, Keith ?, Geoffy Mather, Martin Bell, Steven Clark, Ian Martindale, -?-, Front row: Corren Kozonica, Susan Bates, Janet White, Vivien ?, Susan Haggie, Jillian Coulter, Mrs Forrester, Catherine Collier, Gillian Carr, June Smith, Margaret Blakebough, Lara MacCalaster.

Gordon College in July 1929. Eleanor Alice Rimington moved her school to Gordon Square in the mid-1890s. A successor, Miss Martha E. Manley, took over in 1925. She is seated, wearing a collar and tie, flanked by two teachers, believed to be Misses Cameron and Welch, who shortly afterwards opened Norwood School. At the bottom right is Patsy McConway. In front of Miss Manley is one of the Scholfield sisters.

Gordon College, c. 1930. The council requisitioned the school to house blitzed families. It was still occupied by the dispossessed in 1947.

Whitley Bay Grammar School, *c.* 1914. The need for a secondary school at the town was agreed in December 1908. Hill Heads Farm was acquired by the county council and the school opened in September 1914, in what had been a field north of the farmstead.

Whitley Bay Grammar School in May 1952. From left to right, back row: Miss Lesley Robson, Miss Harrison, Roly Neighbour, Harold Hardman, Leo O'Donnell, Mrs Maureen Lee, Mon. Yeo. Middle row: Mrs Joan Bundred, Doris Louet, Ron Morrow, Charlie Russell, Jim Fawcus, Robin Stewart, Tuffy Seddon, Miss Adelaide Youngson, Madge While, Bill Porter, Fritz Biermann, Dennis Milner. Front row: Stan Holmes, Miss Chrissy Huntingdon, Harry Young, Miss Kate Evans, Nigel O. Parry, George Worsley, Miss Eileen Tinsley, Ted Jones, Morgan Hall. Mr Parry retired in 1952 but returned to Tyneside as a Presbyterian minister.

Whitley and Monkseaton High School for Girls in October 1923. At the left end of the group

of teachers seated at the front is Miss Fairbairn (French); in stripes is Miss Headford (mathematics).

Whitley and Monkseaton Technical School, *c.* 1896. In the interests of improving British industry, Government grants were made to encourage the study of useful arts and sciences. In 1895 the county council rented a room for classes. For the year 1896 this ex-holiday chalet was erected behind the Church School. They offered cookery, woodwork and ambulance courses.

Yearsley, *c.* 1920. Once a private house on Delaval Road, 'Yearsley', with 'Lyndhurst' next door, became part of the Further Education College in 1958.

Seven
The Promenade

Have you ever seen Whitley Bay like this? I have.

Whitley Bay, c. 1914. A favourite novelty postcard emphasized the 'fun' side of the town. Although family holidays to the resort began to decline with the advent of cheap package holidays to the Mediterranean, the clubs and pubs at the coast continued to draw people from the region.

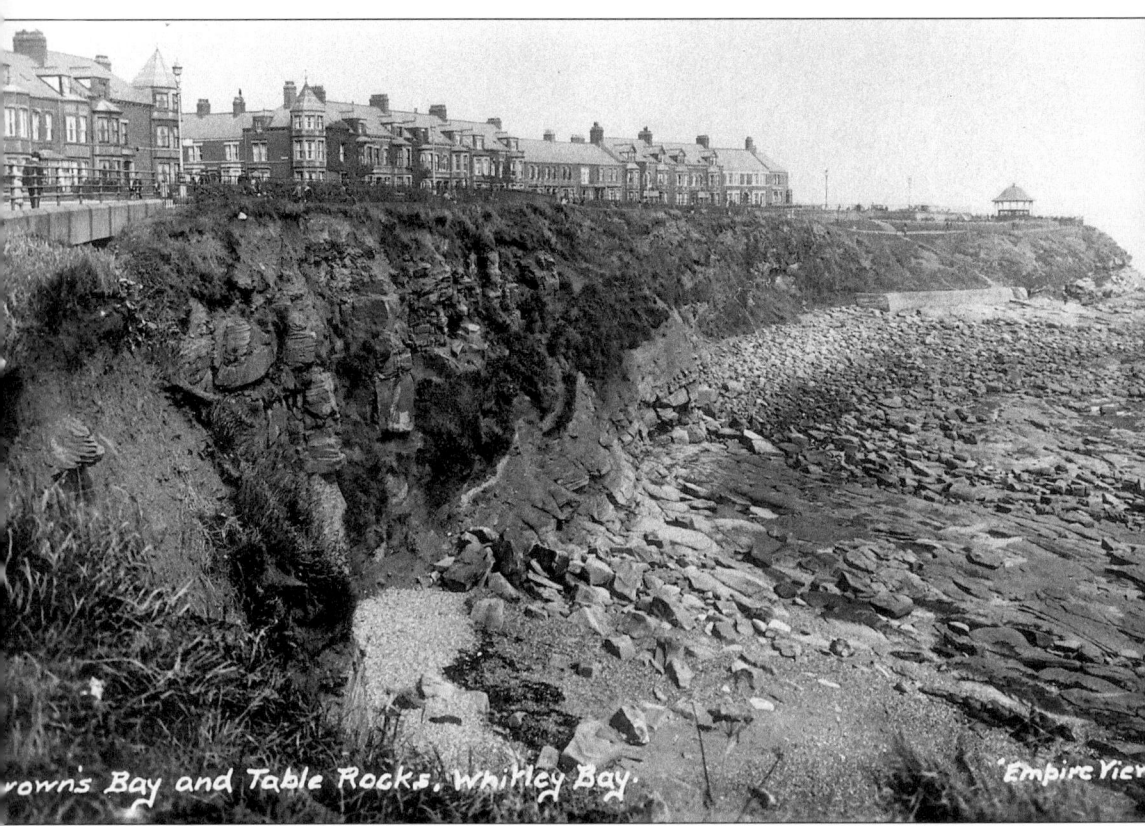

Brown's Bay and Table Rocks, Whitley Bay. 'Empire View'

Brown's Bay, *c.* 1925. Windsor Crescent and Brown's Bay are near the southern edge of Whitley Bay, on the boundary with Cullercoats. In the distance is the bandstand, removed from the Links to Rockcliffe in 1908, with Table Rocks just below. It was from this point, in 1893, that the Local Board of Health began to convert the narrow cliff-top path into a promenade fit for a modern resort. Even while they were building no one suspected that there were old pit workings here, which eventually led to the subsidence of the turreted house at the top left. The promenade was built slowly, in sections. In places the council found that the broad sweep they envisioned was rendered impossible because early builders had left little room near the cliff edge. Significant additions and improvements were made between 1903 and 1908, and by 1911 the main promenade was considered to be complete. As early as 1907, however, there were ambitions to extend the construction to beach level. Starting at the northern end, the council began to work back towards Rockcliffe. The promenade below South Parade and the Esplanade was completed by 1924, and it was carried almost as far as the Table Rocks in 1932. In the meantime large hotels had begun to appear at the seafront and gradually many of the houses were converted to fulfill the same purpose.

Table Rocks, *c.* 1930. On 27 July 1894 W. Scott applied for permission to construct a swimming pool at Table Rocks. C.H.M. Robson claimed it as his idea, costing £200, with £28 by subscription. The council refused to reimburse him, but doubled the size of the pool in 1908.

Young Women's Christian Association, *c.* 1918. The Cliffe Hotel, at 2 Rockcliffe Gardens, opened as a YWCA home on 8 November 1912. It was there through the 1930s, but in 1940 became Griffin's temperance hotel, and later the High Point.

Victoria Gardens, *c.* 1910. Known as Muir's Gardens in the 1890s, the slope lay below Victoria Avenue. Percy Road, to the left, was built in part by Alfred Styan, who complained in 1878 that if the council did nothing the houses would wash away.

Southern Lower Promenade, *c.* 1930. With help from the Unemployment Grants Commission the promenade was extended below Percy Road and Rockcliffe Gardens. Behind the sea wall the paddling pool replaced a suggested swimming bath.

The Promenade, Whitley Bay.

Redcar House, *c.* 1910. The turreted house was Alfred Styan's home in the 1880s. From around 1890 it was an hotel, known variously as Promenade Hotel, Bawtree's boarding house, and the Grand Temperance Hotel.

Alfred Styan, 1840-1902. He came to Whitley in 1868 and set up as one of the earliest developers. Beginning with St Mary's Terrace, he went on to work in Percy Road, Victoria Avenue and Whitley Road.

Corkscrew Stairs, 1910. The Empire Cinema was built in 28 days, to open 20 June 1910. It closed as the Gaumont in 1960.

Pier, 1910. An Act of Parliament was passed in 1908 to allow the pier to be built and this sketch appeared in the company prospectus. It was to be built at the foot of the Esplanade, to measure 802 feet long and 35 feet wide, with a concert hall and shops. The scheme failed, but the idea was revived in 1935. Discussions with the council were still taking place in the 1960s!

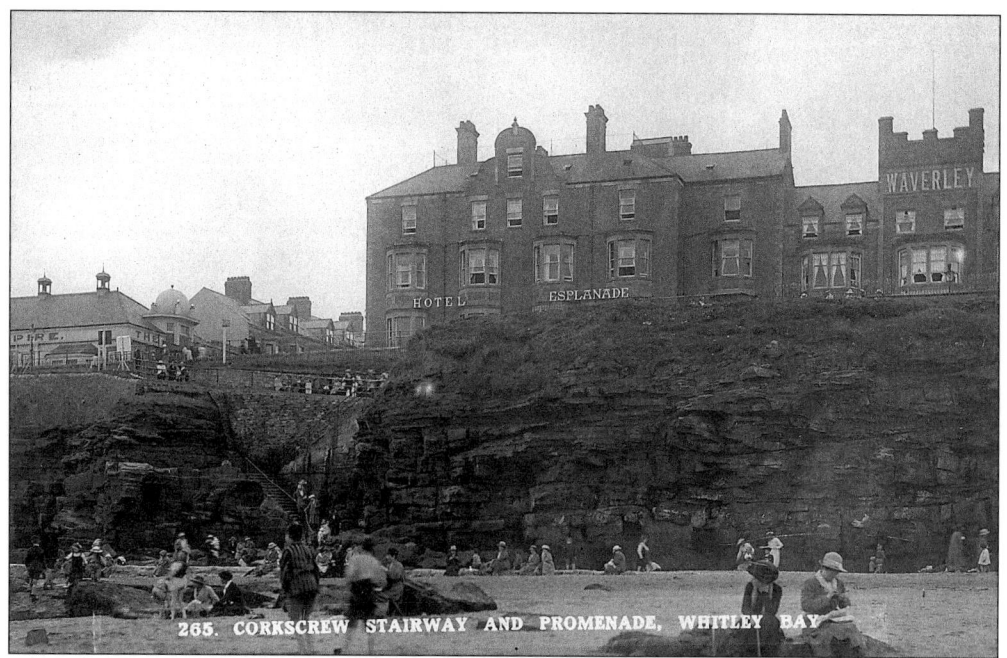

265. CORKSCREW STAIRWAY AND PROMENADE, WHITLEY BAY

Esplanade Hotel, c. 1920. The hotel was begun at the foot of the Esplanade, overlooking Corkscrew Stairs, in 1902. Originally there was an open space next door, where the Waverley Hotel was built a few years later.

Corkscrew Stairs, *c.* 1913. The Waverley was part of a chain of temperance hotels in the North of England. It opened on 21 June 1907. Gradually the neighbouring houses were absorbed, a second tower being added around 1912.

Waverley Hotel. In the 1920s the Waverley was described as one of the largest, most luxurious and most up-to-date hotels on the north east coast. It had about 150 bedrooms and its own heated garage. To the rear, there was a private tennis court.

Waverley Hotel, *c*. 1935. New electric lighting, described as the 'last word in brilliant illumination', was introduced to the promenade in 1924. During the mid-1930s the seafront used extra strip lighting during summer months.

Rex Hotel, *c*. 1939. The Waverley eventually took in all the neighbouring houses and expanded over the open ground as far as South Parade. In 1937 it became the Rex Hotel. Below is the roof of the theatre on the lower promenade.

Grant's Clock, c. 1935. 'A little sister to the Lighthouse', was how Lady Gregg described Grant's Clock, unveiling it on 12 April 1933. Whitley Bay's first town clock was presented to the town by Councillor James Hamilton Grant, vice-chairman of the Urban District Council. It was powered by batteries in the Waverley.

The beach, 24 August 1907. This, the first sandcastle competition at Whitley Bay, was credited to H.L. Evans, draper. The winners were M. Cross and Rowland Wood in the boys' classes, and Vera Davy and Lilian Hanscomb of the girls'.

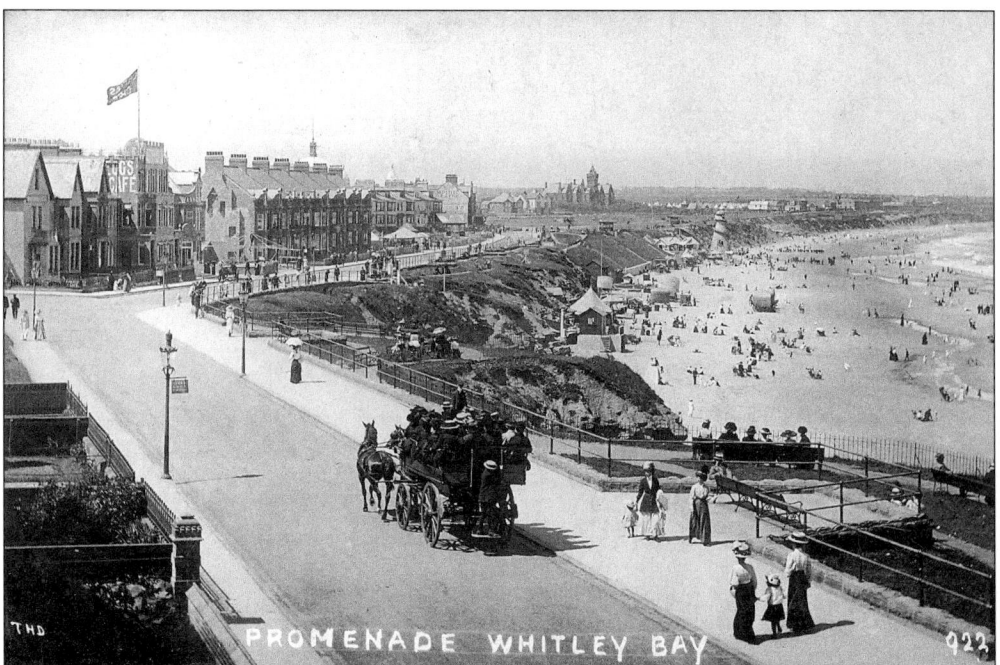

Promenade, c. 1912. Sir Henry Gregg lived behind his café, to the right of Manor House. It opened in 1905, and is here much enlarged. Gregg was mayor of Tynemouth between 1914 and 1918, and was knighted for his war service.

Promenade, c. 1935. Manor House has become a shop, and the Broadway Café has been built on the far side of Gregg's. Nancy Anthony set up the open-air theatre on the Central Lower Promenade in 1930.

Dunn's Tea Rooms, *c.* 1958. John Dunn was one of the earliest providers of facilities on the beach. He died in 1924, shortly after opening his café on the lower promenade. The family kept up the business into the 1960s.

John Dunn, 1835-1924. In June 1868 he erected a tent on the beach and began to charge for changing facilities, the first at Whitley Bay. Two years later he bought his first five bathing machines from Tynemouth.

Bathing machines, *c.* 1911. John Dunn's machines, drawn into the sea by horses, provided privacy and comfort. He lost two to storms in 1881, but there were eighteen at this time.

The beach, *c.* 1908. The Esplanade and Waverley Hotels have been built, but the Empire Cinema is some time in the future. East Parade, to the right, is incomplete. Gregg's Café is still partly a converted house, and the Royal Hotel is not yet begun.

The Sands, Whitley Bay.

Gregg's Slope, *c.* 1913. There were often fatalities among the swimmers, and those who took out the hired boats. In 1911 rescue equipment was installed in the hut at the foot of the slope which took its name from Harry Gregg's palatial café.

Dedication of New Patrol Boat, Whitley Bay.

Gregg's Slope, 25 May 1912. Four boys were swept off the Corkscrew Stairs in the previous year. Councillor A. Nicholls had W.H. Fry build a beach rescue boat which was formally launched at the beginning of Whit weekend.

PROMENADE AND SANDS WHITLEY BAY.

Promenade, 1914. While East Parade, to the right, was being built, Lancelot and Annabella Turner had the Grand Temperance Hotel, beside the Empire. In 1911 they opened two converted houses in the centre of East Parade as the Royal Hotel.

Promenade, 1935. The beach is cluttered with the mobile slipways for Fry's boat trips. In the distance is the enlarged New Empire cinema. It became the Gaumont in 1950, and was later the Alletsa Ballroom.

Brook Street Gardens, *c.* 1910. Around this period W. Catlin was seeking permission to build a Kursaal for his concert party. He hoped to erect it at the far side of the gardens, but the council turned down his applications.

Priory Café, *c.* 1938. Dissatisfied with the cramped offices at the park, in July 1937 the council opted to build new offices on the site. Pending action, they voted to take a lease on the Priory Café in December 1938.

Park Avenue, *c.* 1913. The gardens between Brook Street and the park were declared to be too old-fashioned in 1938. It was suggested that the old iron railings be removed, and the conveniences filled in.

Promenade, 27 May 1911. An overcast Saturday saw the official opening of the promenade. The Duke of Northumberland stood on a platform covered with red cloth, performed the ceremony, and walked the council down to tea at Rockcliffe School.

Promenade, 27 May 1911. The crowd at the official opening was controlled by Boy Scouts and the Church Lads' Brigade. Entertainment was provided by the Percy Main North Eastern Railway Silver Prize Band.

Promenade, 27 May 1911. This was the last public appearance of Thomas Thompson, the 'Father of Whitley', who worked in Whitley's local government for sixty years. He died at Hill Heads Farm, in the same bed where he was born in 1825, on 5 October 1911.

Eight

Local Groups

Wansbeck Division Unionist Association, c. 1929. Viscountess Ridley is presenting the first prize at a whist drive to V. Thompson, at the Empress Ballroom. The town supported a wide range of political, charitable and leisure groups, who kept the hotels and dance halls busy with meetings, dinners and fundraisers.

T.S. 'Whitley', 14 April 1954. The Princess Royal's visit on Charter Day brought local organizations out in force. Mr S. Pearson, the princess, Lord Allendale, Councillor Charlton, the Charter Mayor and Irene Ward MP are welcomed by the Sea Cadets.

Red Cross, 14 April 1954. At the Rex Hotel the princess was greeted by members of the local branch of the organization.

13th Whitley Bay Wolf Cubs, *c.* 1930. Edith and Pat Mayhew of Marden House formed the St Paul's church troop in 1929. With them is Revd F.H. Dowland. Laughing at the back is W. Taylor, with A. Robinson in front of him.

North East Coast Art Club, *c.* 1935. Through the 1920s and onwards the club held annual exhibitions in Whitley Bay. The area has long inspired amateur and professional artists.

Evans & Co. staff outing, 15 July 1914. Harold L. Evans established his long running fancy drapery in Whitley Bay around 1905. A caption on the original picture notes that the shop ran an annual trip to the Morpeth area. The charabanc is outside the shop at the corner of Whitley Road and Trewitt Road. The smiles of pleasurable anticipation on the faces of some of the passengers would no doubt soon be tempered by the realities of a long journey along old country roads at a steady 25mph in a vehicle with solid tyres and limited weather protection. The day's events were reported in the *Whitley Seaside Chronicle and Visitors Gazette* of 18 July. The party, numbering about fifty, proceeded to Bothal Woods where, after what is described as 'a sumptuous repast', everyone proceeded to the sports field to take part in ten events, prizes being presented by Mr and Mrs Evans. Breaking the return journey at Morpeth for refreshments, the party eventually arrived home, tired but happy at 10.45p.m. and showed their appreciation in what is described as 'very hearty manner'.

Front Street, *c.* 1920. Alderman John Thomas Porter of North Shields is at the wheel of the lead car. Apparently this was a day trip he had organized, to visit the coast.

Miss Cormack's school, 9 September 1922. Barnardo's was the first flag day to be officially opened. The pupils, led by Mrs Milton, are in the uniform of St Paul's church Girl's Brigade. They include Elizabeth Lane, Joy Milton, Betty Renton, Pauline 'Popsy' Clarke, Jenny Dinsdale, Isa Simpson, Gertie Athey and Dorothy Hearou.

Whitley and Monkseaton Carnival Committee, *c.* 1929. It is June, and a crowd has gathered in Whitley Park to watch the dancing tableaux at the garden fête. Various gambling booths can be seen in the background.

Table Rocks, 24 September 1910. The newly formed Whitley and Monkseaton Bathing Club, otherwise The Winkles, watch Councillor Dowling open their club houses on the cliff above the pool. A film was made for Grice's Pavilion Electric Theatre.

126

Sandcastle competition, 19 August 1908. There were 232 entries, competing in six classes. As card 14 is labelled 'Boys Age 12 to 15' the boy with the trowel is presumably A. Gibson, son of Mr Thomas Gibson of 45 Countess Avenue.

Sandcastle competition, 19 August 1908. If these are the winners of the girls' class for 9 to 12 year olds, then they are D. Freeman of 36 Charles Avenue, N. Davy of 32 South Parade and E. Martin of 41 Beach Avenue.

Sandcastle Committee, 1908. The Whitley Advertising Committee organized a number of sandcastle competitions during the summer of 1908; these are the members and officials who ran them. Councillor W.L. Dowling, chairman of the Links and Sands Committee of Whitley and Monkseaton Urban District Council is in the centre, and on the left Councillor Robert White is placing a coin into a young lady's collecting box. It is known that other judges included Councillor R. Tulip, J. Moore, M.R.F. Bradley and J.F. Rose. They presided over the second competition, on the 19 August 1908, which saw the sands of Whitley Bay moulded into castles, houses, churches and various animals. The contestants were divided into classes by age and sex, with two special prizes being awarded for the best entries overall. These were won by E. Barker of 1 Albany Gardens (boys 9 to 12) and M. Murton of 5 Victoria Terrace (girls 12 to 15). The prizes were awarded that evening at Catlin's pierrot stand, by Councillor Mason. As the advertising committee was a voluntary organization dedicated to making Whitley Bay widely known as a resort, a number of young ladies wandered the sands with collecting boxes during the competition. The prize of a pair of gloves, for the most money collected, went to Miss L. Bonner.